Walk With Me

Mind-shift from a negative mindset to a positive mindset,
because you said you would and it equals results
#WarriorsMindset#Thestayfocusedmovement

REGELINE EDEN SABBAT

Quantity sales special discounts are available on quantity purchases by corporations, associations, and others. For details, contact the publisher at the address above.

Orders by U.S. trade bookstores and wholesalers. Email info@BeyondPublishing.net

The Beyond Publishing Speakers Bureau can bring authors to your live event. For more information or to book an event contact the Beyond Publishing Speakers Bureau speak@BeyondPublishing.net

The Author can be reached directly BeyondPublishing.net/AuthorRegelineSabbat
Phone Number: 1(323)296-9941

Email: Regelinesabbat@lifeservicecenterofamericallc.com
Website: www.lifeservicecenterofamericallc.com

Social Media Handles:
Instagram:@gigisabbat
Snapchat: Spectacular.g
LinkedIn: Regeline Sabbat
Facebook: Regeline "Gigi" Sabbat
Twitter: Regeline _ Sabbat

Manufactured and printed in the United States of America distributed globally by BeyondPublishing.net

BEYOND

New York | Los Angeles | London | Sydney

ISBN: 978-1-949873-71-9

Contents

Acknowledgements

First and foremost, I want to say "thank you" to my amazing publisher, who has become a friend on this new journey I have embarked on. Michael Butler is absolutely wonderful. He has been so supportive since the start of me writing my book. His words of encouragement, and when he told me, "I knew you could do it," truly touched my heart. I will forever be grateful for Michael Butler, because he has made my dreams come true, and I am able to begin walking with all of you because of Michael "Holding On". Michael has truly been patient with me and understanding. This experience has been so surreal thus far; however, with Michael's support, I have been able to push through the major hurdles in order to get my story out to all of you. From deep within my heart, thank you, Michael.

I truly recommend Beyond Publishing, if you are considering having your book published. Michael Butler is remarkable and genuine, and he will assist you every step of the way.

Thank You so much to the beyond publishing team. I truly appreciate all of you and your assistance with publishing "Walk With Me".

Thank you so much, Andy Audate, for being genuine, an amazing mentor, and friend. You are truly an angel. I am grateful for you giving me the opportunity to be a part of your Elite Presenters Academy. I definitely see the progression in my life since completing the EPA. I truly recommend attending Andy's Progression Conference and the EPA, if you are ready to take action and experience accelerated progression. Also, Thank you so much to the Progression Conference team.

Thank you so much to my lovely parents, who have stood by my side during this major transition in my life. I love you, Mom and Dad. I have watched both of you work so hard to provide for your family, and I will forever be grateful.

Thank you to my brothers, Richard Sabbat and Jeffrey Sabbat. You both are your sister's keeper. And, I am truly my brother's keeper. I love both of you.

I am grateful for the following individuals support on my journey:

I am grateful for the Sabbat Family, the Duplan Family, the Toussaint Family, the Etienne Family, the Beauzil Family, the Goldwire Family, the Georges Family, the Montas Family, the Alkhatib Family, the Bonilla and Aguilar Family, the Melan and Martinez Family, the Quintana Family, the Barquet Family, the Nash Family, the Smith Family, the Zapata Family, the Daniels Family, and the Bandy Family.

I am grateful for Donya Alkhatib, Kelis O'Rourke, Brittany Corfman, Linea Knox, Amy Ford, and Keyanntae Miller.

A special thank you to Brittany Corfman. You are truly an angel.

I am grateful for Team Trump, Team Rubio, CLC, RPOF, JMI

I am grateful for Carly Buonanducci (CWA), Clarice Henderson,

I am grateful for my friends from ITMS, MHS, BCC, VCC, SJA, EBG, WMU, HDC, UCF, ALU, AFP, NWM, EPA, and the PGI.

In loving memory of Mommy YouYou, Papi Pierrot, and Uncle Carlot.

Thank you for your love and support in my life.

I truly love all of you.

Love is patient, love is kind. It does not envy, it does not boast, it is not proud. It does not dishonor others, it is not self-seeking, it is not easily angered, it keeps no record of wrongs. Love does not delight in evil but rejoices with the truth. it always protects, always trusts, always hopes, always perseveres. **1 Corinthians 13:4–8**

Let Go Let God

Family

True Friendship/ Genuine and Unconditional

True Friendship/ Genuine and Unconditional

Health & Nutrition

Volunteering/ Giving back to my community

Writing this book took a lot of pushing through, but I am happy to tell you here I am, "because of "you". Thank you.

Imagine for many years, you obtain knowledge while attending school or you obtain knowledge by being an active member in your community, and you spend so many years helping others one by one and pushing them to be leaders, not because you have to, but because you want to, deep down in your heart.

*"Leaders become great not because of their power, but because of their ability to empower others." - **John C. Maxwell***

Then, after you realize the effect you have on one individual's life, you witness God's love, then you continue walking with God, and you continue pushing others to be leaders, but then you reach a point where they all want the same thing, which is for you to be next to them as they lead. I am grateful for each of you—you know who you are.

Even after I kept pushing others, because I truly cared and I saw the beauty in each of them, they still didn't want to walk forward without me.

I spent time reflecting, and after I reflected I decided, there is someone who needs to hear my story.

Then, I decided I will no longer lead without teaching the best way I know how, and that is by truly being myself, which is to lead by example, no matter what. Imagine an individual with years of knowledge obtained, sitting in a chair on the beach, watching the waves, hoping and praying for change in our beautiful world, watching so many individuals walk by, and the individuals who stopped along the way, you communicate with, and those communications you have with those individuals are beautiful, but I always thought about the individuals who I didn't have the chance to communicate with. I am so happy, I decided to get up, and walk with "you", because waiting does not create change, action creates change. Let's walk together.

By being myself, therefore, requires me to come forward in a way I have never done before, because all my life, I wanted to make certain others saw the beauty in themselves, because I wanted everyone to know, beauty is truly in the eyes of the beholder, and that our world is only as beautiful as we make it. I truly believe, there are infinite/positive innovations we can create and implement during this lifetime in our country. After all, if we don't now, who will?

Our future generation is truly only as strong as we make it. Walking together with God (or the person or thing) we believe in guiding us on our stay-focused movement is the only way.

Therefore, after reflecting with prayer, I realized in order to help others the best way I know how, I had some progression to do in my own life, and that it's okay, because in this lifetime, as long as we do not give up in all areas of our lives, we have the ability to grow.

Growing in all areas of our lives one step at a time is truly possible. We may be faced with trials and tribulations along the way on our journey, but once we keep pushing through, at the end of the tunnel, there is a light. I promise you, there is a light, and it is so beautiful.

Walk with me, and let's bring our world back together. The only way is forward.

Therefore, let's walk together one step at a time and one day at a time.

Introduction

I am Regeline Eden Sabbat, but I prefer Gigi for short. I was born on March, 22,1993 in Coral Springs, Florida. I am trilingual. I speak English, Haitian Creole, and French.

My parents, Guerline and Reginald Sabbat, came to the United States of America in the 80s, from Haiti, which is known as the poorest country in the world. My mother and father were both born in Jacmel, Haiti. They have three children. My eldest brother, Richard Emmanuel Sabbat, and my older brother Jeffrey Sabbat, and myself.

My parents combined their names together— Guerline and Reginald— to create my name: Regeline.

My grandmother and my grandfather on my mother's side were teachers in Haiti, and they both came to the United States of America and lived in New York in the early 70s, in a pursuit of a better life for their family.

My grandmother and my grandfather on my father's side remained in Haiti raising their children.

My grandparents always made certain my family and I were brought up on the same core values they were taught, which is to treat others with respect, the same way we want to be treated, and that hard work requires action daily. My grandparents explained to us in chronological order: God (the person or thing you believe in to be your definition of God), family and genuine friends, work, and then everything else is significant, because in this order, your life will have balance.

Having balance in your life is essential to living your life with no limits. When life throws obstacles on your path, find a way around it, similar to the way you find a way to unlock a door that is locked, by first believing that you can, and essentially what you end up doing is finding a way to do so, because you know you can.

Once you believe in yourself, then you can do anything you set your mind to do, which is a phrase my parents would tell my brothers and I growing up, that we could "do anything we set our minds to do".

I'll never forget my Great-Aunt Mommy You You continuously repeating the terms "dix-sept jour", which means seventeen days in French. Growing up my Great-Aunt Mommy You You, often told me "dix-sept jour", because she wanted me to grow up and to never forget, how after I was born she took me into her arms and took me to Haiti with her.

My Great-Aunt Mommy You You took me into her arms and with her to Haiti, because she wanted my mother to focus on school and get her nursing license.

My mother completed nursing school and today she is an RN and OB nurse, and she teaches neonatal courses. My family and I are so proud of her.

Moreover, my mothers work ethic impacted my life tremendously. Observing my mothers work ethic growing up, provided me with the knowledge and the work ethic in my life, because my mother is truly my role model.

Furthermore, my Great-Aunt Mommy You You assisted my parents a lot. I recall when I was thirteen years old, and my family and I went to visit Mommy You You at her house in Haiti. Mommy You You opened the front door, and as always she had a huge smile on her face, and I'll never forget she said " Regeline, you're older now, let me show you around the house", then as she showed me around the house, we reached a location in her house, that caused Mommy You You to stop walking for a moment, and i'll never forget the look on her face as she looked around, and then she said to me " Here it is, this is my garden, and I want you to never forget it". I'll always remember, because in her garden as we sat down, she shared a part of her life story with me.

Mommy You You told me after she took me in at "dix-sept jour", she traveled back and forth with me from Haiti to America, to allow my parents to be able to spend quality time with me. Then, she told me at three years old my father wanted to bring me back to America, because my brother Jeffrey and I got terribly bit by the mosquitoes in Haiti, while playing in the backyard. Therefore, upon my brother Jeffrey and I returning to America with my father, he made the decision to support my mother while she went through school, and he worked small jobs to provide for his family.

Once my mother graduated nursing school and began working at the hospital, my mother told my father to follow his heart, because she knew for so many years, his heart wanted to spend quality time with his father in Haiti.

My Grandfather and my father were very close and when my Grandfather passed away, my father took it very hard. Therefore, a lot changed in the Sabbat household.

After my Grandfathers passing, my dad always traveled to Haiti about 3-5 times a year. My brothers and I knew our father was happy to spend time in Haiti and give back to his community through his band and his business, so growing up we didn't mind him traveling to Haiti. My father always told my brothers and I he loved to travel and when we grew up, he planned to take us with him.

I thank God every day, that one day I finally had the courage to ask my father, if he may please stay with my brothers and I for Christmas, because I had a feeling in my gut, that something, as I reflect back on this memory, as I share my story with "you", I know God was walking with my family as he continues to do so today, because had I not followed my gut and intuition, my family and I may have never seen my father again.

Normally my father traveled to Haiti after my mother's birthday (December 2nd) and right before Christmas, and he normally remained in Haiti for his birthday (January 2nd), and he always returned before my birthday (March 22nd).

On January 12, 2010 I recall hearing my parents scream out loud to my brothers and I " hurry come and see what is going on", my brothers and I rushed to my parents room, and it was at that moment, we received the news of the earthquake in Haiti.

My father built a five story and a two-story house in Jacmel Haiti. And, on the fifth floor, a location of the house where my family and I had memories together of viewing the beach, unfortunately on January 12, 2010, we observed it collapsing before our eyes. However, as the house was being destroyed, we received news my Grandmother on my father's said, was in the house, when the earthquake hit Haiti. My family and I began to panic, because the first story of our family house in Haiti, had completely went into the ground.

My father's jeep in the ground, instruments for his band, memories with his father and loved ones, our memories, furniture, and his small business that provided beverages to the individuals who worked in food markets around his home on the street completely shattered. However, my parents always taught my brothers and I, material things are just things, that may be replaced, but " life you can't replace". Therefore, my family and I were focused on the safety of my Grandmother, and we continued to hope and pray that she was safe.

A porch door that had bent backwards on the first floor saved my Grandmothers life, because it kept the second floor from falling any further on my Grandmother. My family and I thank God, my Grandmother survived and by the grace of God, she stood up after being pulled from the rubble.

My father obtained footage and an individual who was passing by on the street in Jacmel, Haiti recorded and gave the film to my father.

On the footage we heard the citizens and individuals who worked nearby, screaming and shouting my Grandmothers name and asking her if she is okay.

Watching the footage was devastating, but then a miracle happened, because we observed my Grandmother responding and being pulled out of the rubble from our house in Haiti, that collapsed. When my Grandmother stood up, she had a cut on her arm and a gash on her head, and my family and I are truly grateful she is alive. God is truly great.

Nine years after the earthquake, my Grandmother resides in America with my Aunt, where she continues to focus on moving forward.

As for my Father, he rebuilt the house. Here are a few pictures of the house after the earthquake on January 12, 2010, the location of the house where my Grandmother was pulled out of the rubble when the house collapsed, and the house after it was rebuilt.

Our house in Jacmel Haiti before the earthquake on January 12, 2010

The location of our house in Jacmel Haiti, where my Grandmother was pulled out of the rubble after the house collapsed during the earthquake on January 12, 2010

The house in Jacmel Haiti under construction

The house in Jacmel Haiti nine years later and the third floor is still under construction

The lesson to learn from the story my Great-Aunt Mommy You You shared with me in her garden, my grandmother overcoming the life changing incident that occurred in her life when she almost lost her life during the earthquake, and my father rebuilding the house after almost losing his mother, it can be vividly seen, that it is truly significant to move forward with a positive mindset, in order to overcome difficulties, challenges, or battles you may face during your lifetime. Therefore, no matter what always remember to never give up and keep moving forward.

CHAPTER 1

"No Limits"

I wake up one afternoon in my mother's room, only to see golf balls placed at the bottom of a walker, and my mother attempting to walk. However, at that very moment, she is told by her physical therapist that she would never be able to walk again. I could see the disappointment on my mother's face. I wondered what I could do to help at my age, because I was only ten years old.

My mother's physical therapist told her that she would be back in a few days to try to help her walk again, and as my mother laid back down in her bed, she avoided making eye contact with me, and she slowly closed her eyes, as she had been hurt by the remarks her physical therapist made.

Before my mother could fall asleep disappointed, I told my mother that everything is going to be okay and that she would walk again. My mother looked as if she was thinking, How? Then, I told my mother that as I laid down and watched her physical therapist do her daily routine, that I had learned each and every movement to be able to do them with her.

At that very moment, my mother smiled. Then, I asked my mother if we could make it a daily routine to do the movements together. My mother said "yes."

The next day, my mother woke up bright and early and ready to attempt to use the walker, and I was ready to help her. I noticed two things in that moment: 1) I was willing to help, and 2) my mother allowed it, which is why we were able to see progress each day.

My mother and I worked on her physical movements every day before I went to school and when I returned from school. As for the other medical issues my mother had, such as having a colostomy bag, I'd take the cleaning supplies needed, and I took care of her, as she had given me careful instructions on how to do so.

After a few weeks, I got used to doing the routines with my mother and every day, I'd see improvement and my mother was beginning to glow, because of all the progress she made.

The routines my mother and I did together, began with my mother sitting up on the bed, and then I would get my mother to stand and grip her hands on the walker. As my mom looked at my eyes, she slowly gripped her hands on the walker, and she made several attempts to use the walker to walk.

At first, my mother was only able to grip her hands on the walker, and then she was able to stand while gripping her hands on the walker. Then, she was able to take one step, and after one step, she was able to take another step, and every day, there was slightly more progress than the previous day. Each day that my mother and I saw improvement in her walking, we were so filled with joy and excitement. Then, one day, it was as though I saw a miracle: my mother was able to get up and walk without having to use the walker.

My mother and I never doubted her healing or made any negative remarks while working on her daily routines. We stayed positive and focused on obtaining positive results.

Therefore, since my mother and I shifted our mindset from a negative mindset due to the physical therapist's remarks to a positive mindset, shortly after, my mother was walking again.

Having a positive mindset is significant in life. My mother and I did not place limits on her capabilities we simply looked at obtaining positive results, and because of our positive mindset, we were able to find infinite possibilities.

In this lifetime, an individual can choose to live a "limited life" or an "unlimited life". A limited life is when an individual is confined within limits and cannot go any further than where they already are, or an individual can live an unlimited life, where they are not confined within limits, and they can do anything and everything they set their minds to do. I truly believe everyone can live an unlimited life; however, the key is to have a positive mindset.

Life is truly what you make of it, and when you want something, you have to first decide, is this really what you want? Then, go after it, with "no limits", without doubt, without hesitation, without fear, without negative self-talk, but with a positive mindset and a heart of compassion.

If you want something in this lifetime, I am here to let you know that you are not being selfish— everyone deserves to live their dreams, but you must understand that you must first find balance in your life and make certain that as you are aiming for your dreams, that you also have a heart of compassion for others, to help others along the way, which means that you are selfless.

Understanding that in this lifetime, the balance you have in your life is a science, and naturally you will reach your dreams, but to act as though you don't see others while you are working on reaching for your dreams is not right. Right is right, and wrong is wrong. Words of encouragement to others does not take much, nor does an action to assist in some way.

I have found in the past that many people believe they are in a competition with another person, but the truth of the matter is that, one can't take from you what is destined to be yours. Therefore, I encourage you to go for all that you want in this one lifetime with no limits and maintain a heart of compassion for others by balancing everything in your life that is important to you.

I recall one sunny afternoon as my mother was driving with my brothers and I to bring us to an event we had all wanted to go to for a while. As we were on the highway, my mother noticed a car pulled over on the side of the highway, and the car began bursting into flames. There must have been several cars that passed by, and although they saw what occurred, they kept driving by.

My mother, on the other hand, stopped her car with three children and wanted to go down the hill to help the individual who was crawling on the floor and provide medical aid, since she is a nurse, but the hill was so high my mother literally couldn't climb back up to us if she were to go down. In that moment, my mother was faced with making a reasonable decision.

The decision my mother was faced with at that moment was: 1) to help someone else, leaving her three children in a car on the highway, or 2) she could decide not to leave her children and still make it to the event and help someone else.

By taking the time to balance the facts out and make a quick but reasonable decision, my mother was able to make certain the EMTs were contacted and the individual received the proper assistance on the scene, before leaving with us and still bringing us to the event we had wanted to go to.

This incident made me recall a scene that changed my life from the movie Save The Last Dance when the main character, who is played by the actress Julia Stiles, mother passes away on the highway, while her daughter is auditioning for Juilliard. The scene from this movie is the reason I never rushed my mother to attend any of my events or basketball games growing up, because I didn't want anything to happen to her or anyone in my family.

This scene also had an impact, regarding me asking my friends or loved ones to attend an event for me, because I did not want my friends to rush to attend an event for me, because I didn't want anything to happen to them, either. The one time I wanted to gather my friends and family together was after my graduation ceremony from the University of Central Florida. Even then, I hesitated to do so, even as much as I wanted to see everyone. Therefore, I recall sending the invitation through text, and I let my friends know if they could make it to let me know. I was happy when my friends arrived safely to my place for my celebration, after my graduation ceremony. This is an example of a negative mindset, but I have shifted my mindset to a positive mindset. Stay focused.

Another incident I recall from observing the incident I mentioned before with the vehicle in flames, was when my cousin was ejected from her car seat and she flew under the truck driving in front of her and she died on impact. Always make certain to wear your seat belt, and do not text and drive. This is why I always say to my family and friends, "Drive safe."

Therefore, it is significant to have a positive mindset and to have faith that everything will be fine. Do not have a negative mindset or worry. Remain positive. Stay focused.

Growing up I always looked forward to ballet practice and show days.

I can still recall my ballet instructor on practice days saying, " No eating at a certain time, only water, everyone must watch their weight, and if anyone notices they are gaining weight, then they must eat less, no snacks, and of course there was her favorite phrase " Plie, Plie, Plie,".

It was always practice, practice, practice, and I respected it because I understood practice makes you better. Therefore, during practice I gave it my all.

Then, for the big show days it was make certain your make up is set, tap shoes, ballet slippers, feather bandanna, glittery outfit, and my story began, " Lights camera action."

Everything was absolutely amazing, until I was sexually assaulted by two individuals. I was about 8 years old. This incident changed my life. This incident effected my social engagements, my friendships, and relationships in general growing up. This incident also made it very difficult for me to trust others growing up.

The memories of the incident came and went throughout middle school, and as I got older, the memories began to become clearer and so did the faces of the individuals.

Growing up, I blamed myself. I'd say to myself if I wasn't a ballerina and if I didn't look so pretty maybe this wouldn't have happened to me (I stopped wearing make up until I began college). This is an example of a negative mindset. Positive self-talk matters. If you ever find yourself in the negative self-talk mindset, shift your mindset to a positive self-talk mindset. Maintaining a positive mindset truly matters.

I recall academics and sports keeping my mind off the sexual assault incident that happened when I was about 8 years old. I'll never forget playing baseball, kickball, and basketball in the public parks growing up. However, growing up I developed what society refers to as "anxiety", but I have come to the realization, similar to the way fear doesn't exist, because it is only as real as you believe it to be, the same goes for anxiety, it doesn't exist.

Anxiety like fear is only as real as you believe it to be.

Growing up I tried so hard to keep my heart blocked until now. That was then, this is now. Only Forward.

I decided to share this part of my life after so many years, because someone needs to hear my story, so they too can overcome any incidents or trials and tribulations they have faced or are facing.

I have forgiven both individuals who sexually assaulted me when I was about 8 years old. Forgiveness matters.

I truly hope by me coming forward, in regards to my story and raising awareness in regards to sexual assault, other individuals who may have gone through the same thing, know that I am walking with them and I believe they can and they will overcome what happened to them too. I also want to raise awareness, regarding sexual assault in our country and our community to prevent sexual assault from continuing to happen. I truly believe with God all things are possible. Only Forward.

CHAPTER 2

"*Never Give Up*"

Poem entitled:

"*Never Give Up*"

Walls surround me
That's all I see
All I want is to be free
I scream at the top of my lungs, God
please help me
The back of my mind
Wants to give up
Then, my heart reminds me, that I am
one of a kind
I feel closed in, with nowhere to go
Then, I remember the beauty of life is to
grow
It doesn't matter if you grow slow
Growing is the purpose of life in everyone
It doesn't matter how old you are
The color of your skin,
Your religion
Your political views
The amount of money you make
The car you drive
How many friends you have
How many followers you have on social
media
Your job title
How tall or how short you are
Your gender

Your sexuality
Your age
Your fashion style
Your body structure
The type of music you listen to
Your families culture, or anything else
that our society's education system has
altered our minds to focus on,
Always remember you are in control of
your minds reticular activating system
You focus on what you want to see, hear,
and believe in, therefore growth is in
everyone
Never Give Up
The light may seem dim right now, but all
you need to do is wake up the reticular
activating system in your mind and you
too will realize you are one of a kind
Never Give Up

-Regeline Eden Sabbat

In this journey we call life, having a warrior's mindset is required, to get over the many obstacles you will face during your lifetime.

A warrior is a brave or experienced fighter.

A fighter is a person who doesn't focus on defeats, but, rather, a fighter focuses on overcoming difficulties.

Mindset is the established set of attitudes held by someone.

Therefore, having a warrior's mindset, means you have positive attitudes similar to the positive attitudes of a brave or experienced fighter.

The warrior is in everyone, but you must first allow yourself to free the warrior in your hearts, to then allow your mind and your heart to fight the negativity in your mind, to allow your mind to shift from a negative mindset to a positive mindset.

Once you make the decision to shift your mindset from a negative mindset to a positive mindset, you will obtain results.

Therefore, once you allow yourself to have a warrior's mindset, there is nothing in this lifetime you cannot overcome.

The results you will obtain are the results of a winner, the moment you quit then you have become a quitter, but this time around that will not be you, because today you have made the decision to shift your mindset from a negative to a positive mindset.

Walk with me and you will learn how I obtained a warrior's mindset over the years and the major obstacles in my life I have had to overcome.

My journey began as an unbelievable journey, but I knew with faith anything is possible. Therefore, I mapped out a plan to reach my dreams.

Many individuals told me it was impossible. However, as Mahatma Ghandi said "It always seems impossible until it's done.

I have always dreamed that on this beautiful journey we call life one day everyone's dreams will come true, as long as they stayed the course and followed their hearts, which in turn would guide them to their passion.

When my parents told my brothers and I, we will be moving to a small town called "Palm Coast", I had no idea what to expect, I was a young girl who did ballet, played the piano, did karate, and attended a private school in Fort. Lauderdale. When we arrived in Palm Coast, FL we only saw land, and the city wasn't fully developed yet. However, over the years Palm Coast, FL quickly expanded, and many individuals and their families moved to the city.

Overtime, after my family and I officially moved to Palm Coast, FL, I developed a passion to help others. As the city began expanding, the ethnicity's/nationality's and cultures in the community did as well. I noticed the diversity in Palm Coast, FL and I loved it. Many individuals who moved to the city were from all over the world, and I found the beauty in my community, because of the enormous diversity. Every individual I spoke with was unique in their own way.

Throughout the years I lived in Palm Coast, FL, I learned and embraced the various ethnicity's/nationality's and cultures. I was able to learn about the various ethnicity's/nationality's and cultures, because I listened to others carefully and I became an observer in my community, in hopes to one day be able to find the solution to help others as it relates to everyone equally while still embracing everyone's ethnicity/nationality and culture.

I have spoken to many friends of mine from high school, who said it was unbeknownst to them, they conformed to society's standards by looking, acting, talking, walking, or engaging in activities that met society's standards. I've also been told that some people felt as though, they did not have a choice, but to conform. I am here to tell you, that you do have a choice.

I thank God, I have a special best friend of mines Nicole Aguilar, whom I am the aunt for her and her husband Sammy's beautiful daughter Eliana. Nicole and I met in sixth grade and we have been best friends ever since. During our sophomore year in High School, she once told me that being myself was awesome, her statement stuck with me forever. I cherished her statement, because it kept me aware of society's standards of whom society felt I should be. I was very hard on myself growing up, because I did not want to conform to society's standards of what I should look like, act like, talk like, or walk like. Therefore, my journey continues with me simply being me.

My Best friend Nicole Aguilar and I

I was born in America and my ethnicity is Haitian. In America, I am categorized in the African American group. I do not view myself as being part of any particular groups. I view myself as an individual whose ethnicity is Haitian and I live in America along with other individuals with different ethnicity's/nationality's and cultures, and I love it.

The beautiful attributes in our country, make the diversity we have in America today absolutely amazing. Our country has transitioned, into a country with amazing individuals who have attributes that are not similar, but combined, it is truly what makes America beautiful. The stay focused movement is for everyone. Therefore, we will continue to walk together along with our diverse attributes, that make us beautiful, because we love it!

The truth of the matter is we were all created to be "ourselves", and none of us will ever be a replica of each other, this is what makes diversity such a beautiful aspect of life, because embracing diversity as it relates to others race, ethnicity/nationality and culture, we are able to see the world around us and everyone in it for who they truly are, and not shut someone out or judge someone because of what society's standards are. I learned this concept very early and very quickly, which allowed me to break down the barriers/limit's others attempted to place in my life.

I allowed my heart to see the beauty in everyone and to truly get to know and connect with everyone for who they truly are.

As Napoleon Hill said "We see people who have accumulated great fortunes, but we often recognize only their triumph, overlooking the temporary defeats they had to surmount before "arriving"

Basically, Napoleon was stating individuals see you in life, but they do not know what you have been through or the obstacles you had to overcome in your life. Therefore, I reach my hand out to you today to walk with me through my journey, as we continue to walk together.

I began attending college in 2011. My first semester of college I attended Broward College in Davie,FL. Then, I transferred to Valencia State College, in Orlando, FL,. I attended Daytona State College in 2012 as a transient student for the summer. Then, I attended the University of Central Florida, and now I am a current law student.

After I graduate law School, I plan to pursue all avenues to help others with the knowledge and experience I have obtained throughout the years.

Over the years I have learned while teaching others, no one ever truly does stop learning, and that is another beautiful aspect of life.

Always remain open to learning and be open-minded. However, do not be easily persuaded, manipulated, or used.

Be gentle, kind, and patient to allow what others are saying to be processed to you, in a way that you are not preparing yourself to respond while others are speaking to you, but you are actively listening, and therefore you are able to respond in a manner which reflects your active listening skills.

The song by Brandon Heath "Give me your eyes", truly made me realize that it's not just me who is vigilant in our world and is an active listener.

My journey through our country's education system, begins when I was in High School, and I began to think heavily about my future, regarding furthering my education, to then help others.

By following my heart, I was able to determine that I will go to college and then I will attend law school, in order to help others.

Then, I was advised in order to graduate with my class, I must pass the math portion of the Florida Comprehensive Assessment Test (FCAT).

I was faced with a difficult decision, because focusing on creating a new action plan to graduate, that would allow me to understand the next steps I needed to take in order to pass the FCAT and complete and pass, the last class I was advised, that I had to pass, required me to develop a warriors mindset, in which I could not give up, no matter what. No matter how many times, I knew in my gut that I would be hit, I had to keep going, because I could not give up on my passion to help others. For me giving up was never an option, because I will not give up on defending and facing each battle head on for my fellow warriors. This is truly the stay focused movement.

Therefore, I shifted my mindset from a negative mindset to a positive mindset, before studying for the FCAT exam.

I recall, sitting down in the office at home, and I wrote down an action plan to graduate.

Every day after school, I stayed after hours on campus to study. I was determined to graduate.

I was a transfer student from the private high school I attended my freshman year, therefore I was also advised that I have a missing course on my transcripts and if I did not complete it, I will not graduate with my class.

While attending High School, I worked Part-Time at Polo Ralph Lauren in St. Augustine, FL. However, I was determined to graduate. Therefore, I maintained a positive mindset.

As I was overcoming one obstacle, it seemed as though obstacles were being thrown on my path, but I knew having a negative mindset will not get me through, therefore I stayed positive and I kept moving forward. I remained focused on graduating.

The process was a challenge, because it was not easy at all. Basketball was my main hobby in high school, but since I had to focus on my academics and shift my studying habits, in order to pass the FCAT exam to graduate, I did not play basketball my senior year.

I recall, after creating an action plan, going to Flagler Beach, FL to think about how I need to find another hobby. I'll never forget my drive back to my house, because on my playlist I had an instrumental for a song come on my radio in the car, and at the time I was driving I didn't make anything of it, but then when I got home and I was contemplating on if I should just throw in the towel in the ring or not, and as I got to my knees, I asked God to please send me a sign. Then, I recall looking up and the light bulb on my desk in my room turned on, and on my desk was a piece of paper. This was an "Aha moment" for me, because I realized what my next hobby was going to be, and that was to write poetry. I also played back the instrumental on my playlist, that played randomly on my drive home that day, and as I began writing, I wrote one poem after the other, and I couldn't stop afterwards. I just wanted to keep writing. I still have my poetry journal as of today.

Poetry became my new hobby and I loved it. Therefore, after studying I wrote poems. I disciplined myself accordingly, and a task that once seemed far out of reach, I knew I wanted to reach it, because that was my main goal my senior year, so I worked hard for it every day.

Breaks didn't exist in my vocabulary. If I missed even a minute of something, I set my mind to do, I was hard on myself, and I made certain I showed up for myself in order to get done what I wanted to get done. Accountability matters. The only person I hold accountable for my actions is myself. Therefore, no matter where you are right now in your life, always remember to hold yourself accountable and maintain discipline in your life and no matter how hard things may seem in the moment, keep moving forward with a positive mindset, and never give up, because if you give up you are only giving up on yourself.

"The first step towards your goals will seem difficult at first, and it's at that very moment you must push through, because once you do you won't ever stop."

-Regeline Eden Sabbat

" Moving Forward one step at a time is absolutely amazing. Continue to move forward, and say to yourself giving up is not an option. Giving up is utilized as an excuse.

Therefore, remove that option and once you have no excuses, then you will move forward."

- Regeline Eden Sabbat

" No matter what keep your head up. Growing is the beauty of life. Every day is a new day to improve in your life. Therefore, keep moving forward. "

- Regeline Eden Sabbat

I will always remember the moment I was in my US Government and Politics course. As I was reciting the preamble to the United States Constitution, to my professor, I was called to the guidance counselors office to receive my results for the FCAT exam.

As, I walked in my guidance counselor's office, she was smiling, and she said to me "you passed the FCAT and completed the last course needed to graduate Regeline."

I will never forget, and I will always cherish the moment, when I was walking out of my guidance counselors office in High-school, she said " Regeline", and when I looked back, she told me to always remember " It is not about where you come from, all that matters is where you are going". This statement remained in my heart and it will remain in my heart forever.

Another moment during high school, I will always cherish is when I went to pick up my cap and gown. The individual at the graduation desk, who was giving the caps and gowns, told me he did not see my name on the list, and he was not expecting me to be on the list. I remained calm as I always do and I said to him " I've done the work sir", he said "I'll be right back" because he had to double check, and when he returned he told me, " You are right, you are on the updated list". Then, because of my height and me being 5'8, he said we have to go outside in the truck to see if he can find the gown to fit me. We then found a gown that fit my height.

My fellow warriors never give up, and never place limits in your life, nor let others do so.

I was able to walk with my high school class in 2011, because I was determined, persistent, and committed. I never gave up.

Regeline Sabbat
"Don't ever quit because that's what cowards do, be a winner and keep moving forward."

Matanzas High School- Graduation 2011

If you are a student at the moment or a future student, prior to taking an exam, always remember a standardized test does not define you. Don't think of a test as a negative task, think of the test as a positive task. Apply the knowledge you have learned. Make certain to read each question clearly and answer each question with the knowledge you obtained by studying.

If you don't do well on an exam the first time, then change or improve your studying habits, to make certain you pass it the next time. However, to avoid taking any test over, give it all you got the first time. Stay focused.

If you have a child/student in high school, make certain to look at the various scholarship options available to students and dual enrollment requirements. This could have an effect on not only the cost of an education, but the years spent to obtain a degree. Therefore, I strongly suggest taking action, regarding this matter, now. Also, make certain your child/student has an action plan in place before the graduation date, to make certain you have an effective approach to reaching your goals and dreams.

Similar to the way, I created my action plan after I was enrolled in the course "legal aspects of business ". During the course, I received the "Most Effective Attorney" and "Best Team Performance" award for the mock trial competition. I loved the course so much it confirmed my decision to attend law school, because I found a way in which I could truly pursue my passion to help others. I will always be grateful for my great aunt Mommy YouYou, because she always believed in me and showed me her support on my journey. Every time Mommy You You visited me from Haiti her and I had discussions of my passion to help others and become an Attorney.

Mock Trial Competition High School -2011

I love you and miss you so much Mommy You You

Mommy You You- Haiti

A life-changing moment for me was when my Great Aunt Mommy You You Passed Away, because prior to her passing away, she attended my High school graduation, and after the graduation ceremony when I went to hand her my diploma, she looked me in the eyes and she said to me " I want your law degree".

I overcame the obstacles I was faced with, by not allowing the negative remarks of others to consume my mind, and I shifted my mindset from a negative mindset to a positive mindset, and I maintained the mindset of a warrior to overcome these major obstacles in my life.

Since I did my research prior to graduating high school, I knew I had the option of becoming a "walk on" to play college basketball after I graduated. Therefore, during the summer after I graduated from High School. I spent hours on the basketball court practicing.

Then, I moved to South Florida to attend Broward College and I'll never forget when I went to speak with the basketball coach. I asked him what the requirements are to become a "walk on" at your college, because although I did my research previously, some colleges had additional requirements, specifically for their school. He told me the additional requirements, and I worked day in and day out to obtain my results to meet those requirements.

However, outside of the basketball court, I was growing in my personal life and I made certain to stay focused on my academics. Therefore, when I spent time with my friends on the team outside of the court, I realized I had to make a life changing decision, so I did.

I learned the entire basketball requirements for the route to the WNBA, and I had my action plan with the steps I needed to take in order to attend law school, of course the route to become an Attorney takes years, but I have never been focused on the numbers/years, I've been focused on the finish line and the hard work it takes to get there, which is by taking one step at a time, no matter what and doing whatever it takes. Law school is truly a marathon not a sprint. Going backwards was never an option, only forward. My mission has and it will always be to help as many people as I can once I do reach all my goals, and along the way I will continue to help others, because that is my passion. Moving forward, even after you get knocked down or back s few steps truly matters. Therefore, utilize the strength within you and keep moving forward.

This was the life changing decision of a lifetime because it was: 1) Continue on a journey towards my dreams of obtaining my Law School degree and giving my Great-Aunt Mommy my law degree, as I had promised her. (Keeping in my mind knowing I will get there, while others kept telling me I couldn't, and also promises and loyalty matter to me) or 2) Heading towards the WNBA route.

If it wasn't for my art class in Broward College and my involvement with being active on campus by being part of the student body organizations, my decision may have been different.

I did a lot of self-reflecting. However, maintaining discipline and obtaining results, after I put in the work was and still is my priority. Therefore, no matter how hard things got, the term "stop" or the words " I can't get up" didn't exist in my vocabulary, because the mind wants what it wants. This means even with sweat, blood, tears, etc, no matter what you keep going forward and you don't give up, you stay focused and you keep moving forward.

I'll never forget my schedule prior to making my life-changing decision, while I was enrolled in Broward college for one semester before moving to Orlando, FL to attend Valencia College.

I had art class in the morning, my gym bag with my basketball and other sports attire in one hand, and my canvass and paint brushes in another bag. After class I had to go to the museum before basketball practice, to complete an assignment for class, and that was fine, because during the hours I spent at the museum, I read architecture books. I came to the realization, that art, architecture, and poetry go hand in hand as far interpretation goes. "Fallingwater", which is a historical landmark in Mill Run, Pennsylvania is one of my favorite home designs, which was designed by Frank Lloyd Wright. His architect designs and the meanings behind them, are powerful, and it made me look at art and poetry in a completely different way. It truly expanded my mindset.

After the time I spent at the museum, I went to the gym at the Broward College campus, I got ready, and showed up on the basketball court on time and ready to go, and every practice I put in the work.

However, the more time I spent at the museum, the more books I read, and the more I wrote for my classes, and the more poems I wrote, lead me to come closer and closer to making my life changing decision.

Then, the day came where I decided to do something I never did before, after I was asked if I wanted to, and that was to share my poem " Let it Go" on the Broward College campus. I shared the poem I wrote "Let it Go", during a student body event, held by one of the organizations, and we had a guest who was a well-known singer, who not only performed that day, but was also one of the judges at the event. I recall her saying " Your up", and I'll never forget I truly " Let it Go", because I gave it my all and I let my voice be heard, by sharing my poem. After my performance, several individuals came up to me and I couldn't believe what I heard. A poem I wrote on a sheet of paper, that I had no intention of sharing, until I was asked to perform at this event, literally had a major impact in several individuals lives. At that moment, I was hit with another " Aha moment".

I quickly went and got changed to go on the basketball court, and the more shots I kept shooting, the more layups I did, and the more drills I ran, lead me to make my final decision. Maintaining a positive mindset truly matters.

I made the decision to keep basketball as a leisure activity in my life and I still have my basketball tattoo until this day to never forget, what lead me to have a passion for basketball back in 6th grade, and that was simply the love of basketball itself. Love is love.

However, I decided to maintain my positive mindset and utilize all of my energy and time into my academics and continue to pursue my passion to helps others. If I had chosen to continue playing basketball, the route to help others the way I know I can would most likely have been after having to play several games according to the "schedules", and that's when I knew that wasn't the route I wanted to continue on, because I wanted to utilize my positive mindset to continue to help others in my country and my community, so I did. No matter what or where I go, I will continue to do so, because my passion is truly to help others. Once you know what you are passionate about and your "why", than you continue to do it because you love it!. Decisions matter. In life you are the pilot of your life, therefore you must navigate your life accordingly and make certain you follow your heart and make certain your decisions are in alignment with your goals and dreams. Stay focused and continue moving forward, no matter what.

Also, I'll never forget my first semester of college, because not only did I make a life changing decision, but besides the classes I attended, basketball practice, going to the museum, and being active in student body organizations on the Broward College campus, I studied for my other classes in the hospital while I visited and stayed with my Great-Aunt Mommy You You in ICU. I am truly grateful for my cousin Sandra Duplan, who traveled all the way from Connecticut to be there as well. Then, Mommy You You passed away right in front of me as I held her hand by her bed side in the hospital. I'll always remember giving her eulogy at her funeral, because as I was speaking, I realized Mommy You You was and still is watching over me and she is in heaven with God.

Furthermore, after making my decision, I moved to Orlando, FL to attend Valencia College.

Recall I mentioned how I decided to keep basketball as a leisure activity, well I did, even when I moved to Orlando, FL. In between work and school, most of my free time was spent on the basketball court.

I'll never forget walking on the basketball court at the public park and I remember the men looked at me and said "Girls don't come around here." And, I said " Basketball is about the game not the gender right, so lets focus on the game, Let's play the game".

Once we got our gender differences out of the way. I recall playing about 5-10 games back to back with my buddies at the Shadow Bay basketball court in Orlando, FL. It was fun, but the reality is once I got off the court, my focus went back to my studies. This is why being disciplined and remaining focused on your priorities is important, so you don't easily get distracted or put off your priorities. Keep going forward.

As far as celebrations go, I truly believe in celebrating once you put in the work to be where you want to be. I don't celebrate while I am in the process of putting in work towards my goals. Let's be honest, what would I be celebrating, if I haven't done the work? Sure, rewarding yourself along the way towards your goal is great, but this is to raise awareness for the individuals who may get distracted or peer pressured when they begin college, to always remember to never lose focus on your studies. My advice is to remember your priorities and before you celebrate, ask yourself, what are you celebrating, and have you truly done what it is you need to do to continue moving closer to your goals and dreams?

My second semester at Valencia college (West Campus), I worked at a restaurant while attending classes and my biology labs on campus (3hrs). Then, after the semester I worked Full-time at a Call Center, that sold discount attraction tickets, and I was promoted to be a Vacation

Planning Specialist at the front desk after a year. During my lunch breaks (1hr) and my fifteen-minute breaks (two breaks a day), I was in the break room with my calculator studying for my courses. Determination matters.

As soon as work was over, I'd go to the math lab at my college, and I was in the math lab until they closed, and on the weekends I would be in the math lab again from the time they opened until the time they closed. Discipline matters.

I disciplined myself, regarding my academic plan, and I made certain to meet with an academic advisor at the beginning, mid-term, and at the end of each semester. Commitment matters.

The mornings I planned to meet with an academic advisor, I woke up early since the lines tend to get long. For example, if an individual were to show up around the time the advisors opened the doors, then the individual had to wait a long time, because for some reason, everyone decided to show up at the exact time the advising department opened. I used to sit down on the floor since my legs got tired from standing at the front desk at my hospitality job, because I worked ten hours a day sometimes five days a week.

Therefore, as I was waiting for an advisor to arrive to open the door, unfortunately sometimes I'd fall asleep on the floor.

However, I was determined to graduate, and I kept a positive mindset.

The lesson here is if you are a student then you should be meeting with your advisor often, your advisors are there to assist you.

If you ever receive any remarks from an advisor that you feel may be discouraging, take it as encouragement to work harder, and always maintain a positive mindset. Whatever it takes you can truly make it through. Make certain to understand 1) your graduating requirements for the degree you want and 2) have an academic plan with the courses you plan to take each semester. View both documents often, until you graduate.

Also, whether you are graduating from a state college, a university, or etc., always remember you did the work to walk across the stage, so if you want to walk across the stage, just know I support you and I am walking with you across the stage. I believe in you.

Valencia College- Graduation 2015

I cherish the moment I went to pick up my cap and gown to graduate from Valencia State College.

I never gave up. As a result, I graduated from Valencia State College and then I transitioned to the University of Central Florida.

Never give up on yourself. If you believe in yourself, then you too can live an unlimited life. I truly believe you are a warrior.

Furthermore, after graduating from Valencia State College, my journey continued when I attended the University of Central Florida, and I obtained my Bachelors of Arts degree in Political Science (Pre-Law) and Sociology, while interning for the United States Senate office.

My final semester at UCF, I took six classes, and when I went to pick up the books for my final semester in the library, the individual at the cashier looked at me and said " You have a lot of books here, you must like to read, I never saw anyone get so many books for one semester." I realized in this moment; I had embarked on a journey I was truly committed too. At the end of the semester I was named to the Dean's List in the College of Sciences for the Summer 2016 Semester in recognition of Outstanding Scholastic Achievement.

The University of Central Florida 2016 - Graduation

" No matter how many times you get knocked down by challenges in your life, always remember to get back up. Shift your mindset from a negative to a positive mindset.

If you didn't get something right the first time, then you get back up and you keep trying, give it all you got. Results will show in your life, when you put in the work."

- *Regeline Eden Sabbat*

The University of Central Florida 2016 - Graduation. My Great-Aunt Mommy You You walked across the stage with me. Walking across the stage and obtaining my Bachelors of Arts degree in Political Science(Pre-Law) and Sociology, I became the First-Generation College Graduate in my family.

Graduating from the University of Central Florida, I cherish the moment I went to pick up my cap and gown, similar to picking up both items for my High School graduation and from the State College, because the journey to reach my dreams that once seemed so far out of reach quickly approached, and only after three weeks of graduating from UCF, I moved to Tampa, FL to attend Law School.

My first semester of Law School I read the book titled " Law School Confidential; A complete guide to the Law School Experience By Students, for Students" by Robert Miller, and I highly recommend reading this book if you are considering going to law school, or if you are a current student, because it changed my life for the better. I am an entrepreneur today because of this book.

I am the type of learner that wants to know how the entire clock works rather than what time it is, because I prefer to not only be able to tell what time it is, but to be able to explain how the entire system works. I am grateful that I read this book early in my career because in the future I plan to be an Entrepreneur/ Attorney.

Another book I recommend, reading is "The remarkable story of a Human Trafficking Rescuer Ma'am Anna" by Anna Rodriguez.

This way you can become familiar with Human Trafficking, because many lives can be saved just by you becoming aware of the topic, and becoming an active observer in your community, and you can notify the proper authorities once you notice something isn't right.

Similar to the way the flight attendant Shelia Fredrick saved a girl from Human Trafficking by being vigilant in 2019.

"Something in the back of my mind said something is not right,"
-Shelia Frederick

Human Trafficking is an international crime that involves the exploitation of both men and women of all ages, race, and ethnicity's/ nationality's being sold for sex, raped, or abused.

Human Trafficking is an ongoing issue in our community.

Our purpose on our walk is to raise awareness. Awareness+Intervention/ Positive Action=Prevention/Solutions.

The National Human Trafficking Hotline is 1(888) 373-7888.

Law school and the organizations I have been a part of, have truly been a remarkable learning experience. I am the former Class Senator for my incoming class, the former Student Bar Association President (SBA) and the founder for the Caribbean Law Students Association (CLSA).

My vision upon forming the Caribbean Law Students Association and to have it implemented at Western Michigan University Cooley law school, was to involve all Law students and   Caribbean Law Students in activities that encourage academic and professional excellence, and to promote a greater awareness and commitment to the Caribbean community. CLSA is committed to providing networking opportunities for all law students interested in doing business with the Caribbean and its community. The Caribbean Law Students Association, is a learning opportunity for all Law Students who are interested in practicing law in any of the Caribbean countries, to educate students on the laws in each Caribbean country.

I abide by the US Constitution and I will continue to do so in all areas of my life. That is what individuals with a warrior's mindset do, in order to maintain a positive environment in our world.

I truly enjoyed serving my student body and I am glad I chose to do so, because I am happy, I had the opportunity to meet amazing individuals and I was able to connect with every student/colleague and Professor, because together we can create positive innovation in our world.

I will always serve other individuals in our community, with "you".

I have experience in other fields such as social work in which I am the former Residential Manager at the Human Development Center, Inc and I assisted individuals with intellectual and developmental disabilities in 2017. I supervised each client and I made certain that their medical/health requirements were met, and I managed each clients training and reports, and financial budgets. I also provided staff training, monitoring, and location supervision.

I received my certificate of completion for satisfying all the APD- Zero Tolerance-Statewide initiative requirements for the agency of persons with disabilities in the State of Florida, and I am CPR certified.

Per the Health Insurance Portability and Accountability Act of 1996 (HIPPA), which is a United States legislation that provides data privacy and security provisions for safeguarding medical information, my clients now and forever will remain anonymous, because I will continue to obey this law.

" Be strong and courageous! Do not be afraid or discouraged for the Lord, your God is with you wherever you Go."
Joshua 1:9

"Warriors, Never Give Up."
-Regeline Eden Sabbat

On 02/07/2019 I obtained my 2-15 Life, Health and Variable Annuities Agent license.

Currently, I am a law student, and I work as an Interpreter at AD ASTRA, Inc (Haitian Creole and French Interpreter). I am happy to be blessed with the ability to assist medical facilities, government facilities, etc with my interpreting skills.

I also have experience as a Financial Representative and I assisted my clients with comprehensive Financial Planning. How I did that was by creating a unique financial plan for my clients.

Moreover, I completed Andy Audate Elites Presenters Academy in 2019, and now I am a Motivational Speaker. I am grateful for Andy's Mentorship, he is absolutely amazing.

"Multi-skilled individuals do exist, and multi-skilled individuals make strong leaders."

-Regeline Eden Sabbat

Our purpose on our walk is to raise awareness. Awareness+Intervention/Positive Action=Prevention/Solutions.

A few of the hobbies I enjoy are writing poetry, the beach, playing the acoustic guitar, playing basketball, volunteering in my community, horseback riding, riding motorcycles, motocross, jet skiing, nature trails, swimming, museums, the movies, playing pool, sports games, concerts, boat tours, and my new hobby is boxing.

As Sylvester Stallone in the film "Rocky" said:

"The world isn't all sunshine and rainbows. It's a very mean and nasty place. And I don't care how tough you are, it will beat you to your knees and keep you there permanently if you let it. You me or nobody is going to hit as hard as life. But it's not about how hard you can hit, it's about how hard you can get it and keep moving forward; how much you can take and keep moving forward. That's how winning is done."

9 Round – Lakeland, FL (2019)

Furthermore, through all of the obstacles I have overcome, being active and vigilant in my community, I realized the main issues in a household are legal and financial issues. For these reasons, I plan to practice Family law and Estate Planning. My passion will always remain the same, and that is to help others in any way that I can. Although, I have found that the major issues in a household are legal and financial issues, there is nothing that can't be fixed once the problem is determined.

Our purpose on our walk is to raise awareness. Awareness+Intervention/ Positive Action=Prevention/Solutions.

After I graduate from law school, I plan to visit my great Aunt Mommy YouYou and give her a copy of my law degree, similar to the way I visited my great Aunt Mommy YouYou at her grave site after graduating from the University of central Florida and gave her a copy of my Bachelor of Arts Degree.

I will continue my journey with all of you and I will continue to walk with each and every one of you, to show you all that together with a warrior's positive mindset, we can and we will accomplish everything we set our minds to do.

You matter, your goals matter, and your dreams matter,
"Always remember, no matter what to never give up."

- Regeline Eden Sabbat

CHAPTER 3

"Set Goals For Yourself and Have a Clear Why"

Throughout my life I was faced with many obstacles, and the day I had a clear "WHY" to reach my dreams of becoming an attorney and helping others, I decided that I will obtain my Juris Doctor degree, and I will keep my promise to my Great Aunt Mommy YouYou, by providing her with a copy of my Juris Doctor degree at her grave site the day of my graduation. Similar to the way I placed a copy of my Bachelor of Arts degree at her grave site.

I recall placing my Great Aunt's photo on my cap for graduation, so that she can walk across the stage with me when I graduated from the University of Central Florida, and she did as the beautiful angel, she will always be.

I set goals for myself both short term and long term, and I know you will too! By creating your own action plan! I believe in you!

Warriors Mindset Visual Roadmap:

Create a visual roadmap for what you want your life to look like in the next few months (which would be your short term goal), and then one for the next five years (which would be your long term goal). Think of your blank sheet of paper as your canvass and what you draw or write on is the canvass/big picture of what you truly want and where you want to be. Now that you can visualize what you want, now is the time to take action, and reach your goals and ultimately your dreams.

Please complete the form below and after you complete it, read it until you feel as though you can officially say, that you know your why and nothing will stop you from reaching your dreams.

"It is possible to look far ahead. Similar to how it is possible to look far behind, therefore ask yourself what can you do today to continue moving forward. Then take action today towards your goals and your dreams."

- Regeline Eden Sabbat

Action Plan:

What is your "why" in life?
(Ask yourself what makes you wake up in the morning)

_____

Where are you now personally, financially, and professionally?

_____

Are you truly happy where you are or are you wanting to work on areas of your life and invest time in your personal development?

_____

Do you know that you matter?

_____

If your life matters to you, then it doesn't matter what others think, you are not living to please others right?

_____

Therefore, I challenge you to answer these questions truthfully and take action.

Literally write the first thing that comes to mind and don't hold back.

What do you truly want?

_____

Challenge questions:

Where do you see yourself in the next 5 years?

_____

_____

Close your eyes and picture who, what, and where you see yourself in the next 5 years?

_____

_____

Do you want your own family and children?

_____

_____

What are you passionate about?

_____

_____

If tomorrow was your last day, can you say you have worked towards personal goals for yourself?

_____

_____

If not why haven't you set goals for yourself if you matter and you love yourself?

_____

_____

Now, I ask you to list one short term goal that matters to you, and if money weren't an issue what would it be?

Your short term goal:_____

Now, one long term goal (come on just do it, you love yourself right).

Your long term goal:_____

There you have it. Two goals for the year to work towards.

Don't worry I'll be working with you every step of the way. We are walking together. Remember that.

You can do it!

Stay focused

And, remember you matter

I believe in you

> *Now that you have a clear " why", do not limit yourself go after your dreams. Sometimes in life it's as if we are in the vehicle we call life, and we tend to keep the vehicle on park, knowing it won't take us anywhere. Today, is the day you don't keep your vehicle in life on park any longer, remove your foot from the brakes and allow your heart to follow it's dreams, with the positive mindset of a warrior, it's go time place your vehicle/ life on drive.*
> **-Regeline Eden Sabbat**

> *"Plant your seeds through out your life and watch your flowers flourish and your faith grow, because you proceeded on your life journey with a warriors mindset, and you never gave up, and you overcame the obstacles in your life"*
> **-Regeline Eden Sabbat**

CHAPTER 4

"Do What You Are Passionate About"

Now that you have taken action and you have determined a clear why for yourself, it's time to amplify your "why", by determining what you are passionate about.

My passion is helping others, which I determined at a very young age from the story I shared with you in regards to helping my mother walk again and learning/embracing the various ethnicity's/nationality's and cultures in our country, and assisting others in many of the various fields I have experience in such as Social work, politics, law and government, non-profit organizations, and the financial field.

What are you passionate about?

_____

What do you have a burning desire for?

_____

Are you happy with what you are currently doing?
_____(Be honest here, folks)

I knew you could do it! Great Job!

If you are happy great job pursing a job that aligns with what you are passionate about. Keep Going!

If you wrote in the last column above that you are not happy with what you are currently doing, then you are definitely not doing what you are passionate about, but it's fine I am going to help you determine your passion here.

You most likely kept the first two spaces above blank, didn't you? Well it's fine because I am here to tell you that everyone does not learn the same way.

Furthermore, for my folks who wrote you are happy with what you are currently doing and for my folks who left the column blank or said no. The different types of learning models are Visual, Read/Write, Aural, and Kinesthetic. Recall, I mentioned before everyone is unique and diversity is a beautiful aspect of life, well here is another example of how everyone is different.

As a visual learner you prefer for information to be laid out in a manner of which you can see it with your own eyes, and you prefer to use symbols and drawings. This means grab a blank sheet of paper and now try it, draw what you are passionate about. Now, you have determined what you are passionate about.

As a Read/ Write learner you prefer using list and plans. This means list out a few things you are passionate about and attach a set date for you to obtain it, at the end you should determine, which one you consider to be a priority to you, and there you have it, you have determined what you are passionate about.

As a Aural learner you prefer to listen and speak. This means try saying out loud what you may be passionate about, if you have the voice memo app on your phone, tablet, or desk top try recording yourself attempting to determine what you are passionate about, after you have said it out loud and recorded yourself a few times, once you replay your recordings, you will be able to determine what you kept stating the most, and now you have determined what you are passionate about.

As a Kinesthetic learner you prefer a hands-on approach and trial and error, as well as taking action. This means what have you done in the past year constantly, or what is something you have taken action on and took the first step towards? Maybe you haven't taken the first step yet,

but now that I have walked you through these questions, I am sure there is something that sticks out in your mind, and now you have determined what you are passionate about.
I will ask everyone again.

What are you passionate about?

_____

Now that you have determined what you are passionate about, make certain to take the first initial step towards your passion, because it is apparent you absolutely have a burning desire to achieve exactly what you are passionate about! I am proud of you.

It's time to learn the next step to make certain you reach your dreams. Let's reflect on how far you have come so far, regarding your personal development "Beautiful Warrior".

You have set your goals and know your why

You now know what you are passionate about

The next step is you must Stay Focused.

CHAPTER 5

"Stay Focused"

My entire life I had to stay focused. Staying focused and having a warrior's mindset, will get you through the major obstacles you will be faced with in your life. You must stay focused.

I truly believe an individual can be skilled in a variety of fields, as long as an individual is disciplined. If an individual is skilled in a variety of fields and is disciplined, then that makes an individual multi-skilled, similar to the mindset of a warrior. Stay focused.

Therefore, when I state "stay focused", it's because many individuals have a difficulty with completing one task or multi- tasking, or individuals tend to easily get distracted. However, if you want something badly, then nothing should stop you or distract you from reaching your goals. If you ever find yourself losing focus, then pause for a moment and reevaluate where you are now, determine what may be causing you to lose focus, and once you realize what may be causing you to lose focus, make the necessary adjustments in your life. Then, continue to work hard to reach your goals.

Anything less than action towards your dreams is an excuse. You must be disciplined and have balance in your life.

Negative habits can be shifted into positive habits. I always say, "if you know what the problem is, then it is truly possible for it to be corrected."

My entire life I had to stay focused. Being born with ADHD, I have found to be a blessing though. Most individuals presume individuals with ADHD are not focused, but the truth of the matter is that individuals with ADHD are actually more focused then one expects. Therefore, if you know someone with ADHD, don't take their condition as a weakness, it's actually a strength.

Individuals with ADHD are able to pick up on the facts and details very quickly and are able to explain it precisely, because individuals with ADHD are detail oriented.

No matter where you are in your life, always stay focused. And, always remember anything less than action towards your dreams is an excuse. You must be disciplined and have balance in your life. If you fall down, get back up because you have the strength, courage, and mindset to overcome any challenge you are faced with in your life. Never give up on yourself.

From this day forward, promise yourself you will no longer make excuses to take steps towards your dreams. No more limiting yourselves. You deserve to reach your dreams too, and I know you will because you are a warrior and warriors never give up.

Staying focused is more than just a movement, it is a national statement that us warriors never give up.

You will reach your dreams. No more looking in the rearview mirror in your life, only forward!

Let's continue to walk this journey we call life together and climb the infinite mountains together.

This brings me to the next step of the warrior's mindset and the stay focused movement, which is financial literacy to get you through the infinite mountains you will face in this journey we call life.

Always remember you are what you focus on. Maintain control of your reticular activating system in your mind, and don't let life drift you away from maintaining control. Stay focused my fellow warriors.

It is significant in this lifetime for every Individual to have their tool kit filled with knowledge. This requires a warrior's mindset in various areas such as basic concepts for financial literacy, politics, sociology, and the warrior's blueprint.

> " *Never lose sight of your goals, no matter what*
> *and always remember, you matter.* "
>
> **-Regeline Eden Sabbat**

CHAPTER 6

"Financial Literacy"

My conviction for financial literacy and helping others financially grew, when I noticed a pattern of individuals having issues related to financial matters.

One day while networking, I came across a man named Mason and we spoke on the phone briefly regarding financial matters. Then, I spoke with him and his girlfriend Celimar via video chat on zoom, and we discussed our thoughts on a financial video we watched. I was astonished at how three individuals could view a major issue exactly the same. I wondered if there were other individuals who thought just like us. Mason and I scheduled a day for us to meet along with his girlfriend at Starbucks. The three of us spoke for about two hours at Starbucks. The discussion was on financial issues and how it effects households tremendously.

In a household everything is surrounded with finances, such as your bills or when you purchase anything for your home such as furniture, groceries, clothes, shoes, hygiene products, or miscellaneous items, you can't purchase those items without money. Therefore, it is significant to budget and save. A concept that seems easy to grasp right?

Well you see for many individuals that is not the case, and that is okay, because recall our discussion earlier, on everyone learning differently, well that is what happened in regards to financial literacy, because it isn't taught in our education system in a direct way as many individuals want it to be.

The fact that many individuals view money in so many different ways causes so many issues in a household, which often times based on being active and vigilant in our community, the majority of financial issues have led to legal issues.

The day after I met the couple at Starbucks, after class I gave a verbal survey to my colleagues, and I asked them "What are your thoughts on finances and do you have a financial plan aligned for yourself, after you graduate? After, the similar answers I received, I planned a meeting with my colleagues from law school and the couple, and we discussed more in-depth financial issues and how it effects a household.

One of the individuals who joined us named Dan, mentioned how he was a teacher, and if he didn't become an entrepreneur with another stream of income, then he would not be able to provide for his family.

After a few months we took a trip to North Carolina and attended a seminar for the weekend, at the convention center regarding financial literacy. I also spoke with several individuals with various backgrounds in amazing professions, who converted to entrepreneurs or continued working in their profession, but also had another stream of income through their entrepreneur business.

Upon my return from North Carolina, I decided to break down the concept of financial literacy in a way to teach it directly to others.

Therefore, I share with you today the most important aspect of financial literacy that is significant to understand, and that is "in order to obtain financial freedom you must first obtain financial security".

In order to obtain financial security, you must know how to budget effectively, and once you learn how to budget effectively you must maintain your budget.

Budgeting your finances effectively is important, to prepare you and your family for retirement to make certain you obtain financial freedom and maintain it.

A budget is an estimate of income and expenditure for a set period of time.

Saving is the money you do not spend and that you put aside, in for example a deposit account, a pension account, an investment fund, or as cash.

A financial plan includes every aspect of your finances.

I will always remember visiting Haiti with my parents and my brothers, it truly had an effect on how I viewed not only the world, but how I can help form positive innovation, in our world. While, I was in Haiti I remember arriving at the airport thinking about how long the line was, but surprisingly no one seemed agitated or irritated. I watched individuals stand in line, without complaining and who seemed happy they had made it to their country. Patience truly matters.

After walking out of the airport, my family and I got in a vehicle with a man whose name was "horn "in English, I recall asking my parents at the time why is his name "horn", my parents told me, "because he is going to take us up the mountain, and on the mountain there are no street lights, therefore he must push on the horn before he can turn any corners on the mountain, if he doesn't then he will risk getting into an accident." I wondered what this mountain looked like, and once we got to the mountain it was so beautiful, if you recall the movie " are we there yet", that was literally me asking "horn", are we there yet?, I wanted so badly to see the top of the mountain, but then I had an "Aha moment ", remembering to be patient.

In that same moment, Horn said we will be there in a few hours, because I felt as though Horn allowed me to enjoy my own excitement for a little moment and then responded to my question, gave me so much peace at our level of understanding, that I fell asleep for the remainder of the ride.

When my family and I arrived in Jacmel, Haiti, I recall looking at the ground, and wondering why no one had fixed it. I asked my mother "Mom, why hasn't any one fixed the street yet"?. My mother looked at me and said "Because, sweetie they need funding for it".

As my family and I continued to walk to our house in Jacmel, Haiti I began observing the individuals in the street, and I recall stopping in the middle of the street, to look at the beauty in which they interacted with each other, even though they knew they didn't have much to give and they were standing on streets with several pot holes.

I recall being so excited I wanted to walk all over Jacmel, Haiti and begin engaging with others to understand their culture and each individual as they appeared, which was as "Beautiful individuals." Every individual was beautiful in their own way.

I could not wait to walk with everyone, once I got out of my comfort zone, I had to push through, because I used to be what America categorizes as an "introvert", but now I am what America Categorizes as "ambivert".

An ambivert is an individual who has the personality, that reflects the balance of extrovert and introvert features.

An introvert is an individual who comes off shy, but is not necessarily shy, the truth of the matter is introverts prefer to be alone sometimes to collect their thoughts, but they don't want to be alone all the time.

An extrovert is an outgoing individual.

Therefore, I am so happy I got out of my comfort zone because it allowed me to build positive relationships in Haiti. I got to know each individual for who they truly are, which are "beautiful individuals", just like you and I in America.

I observed how the individuals engaged with each other, they were humble/respectful towards each other, and I loved it. The smiles I observed after one kind act each individual did for another, was truly beautiful. Another beautiful aspect of what I witnessed was, they expected nothing in return from each other, and I loved it.

Expect nothing and you will never be disappointed.

- Unknown

Moreover, understanding an individual's love language is truly significant, because our features that are not similar to each other, is what makes our country beautiful. As Gary Chapman mentions and explains in his book " The 5 Love Languages", understanding each love language is truly important.

The five love languages are Words of Affirmation, Acts of Service, Quality Time, Giving gifts, and Physical Touch.

Take action now and discover what the various love languages mean.

Words of Affirmation:

_____
_____
_____

Acts of Service:

_____
_____
_____

Quality Time:

_____
_____
_____

Giving Gifts:

_____
_____
_____

Physical Touch:

_____
_____
_____

I also highly recommend taking the five love languages. There are several quizzes, such as the couples quiz, children's quiz, singles quiz, and teens quiz, and etc, to understand the love languages for each checkout the website: *https://www.5lovelanguages.com/quizzes/*

After taking the 5 love languages quiz, my significant other and I were able to understand each other's love language better, and we have built on our relationship ever since. We place God first in our relationship, and I love it.

"Be the change that you wish to see in the world."
-Mahatma Gandhi

This quote by Mahatma Gandhi has always stayed in my heart, because through my observations in Haiti, I took time to determine ways I could not only help others in America, but ways I could also help the individuals in Haiti, so I took a walk with the individuals in Haiti who wanted to walk with me, it was then I realized, there are other individuals love language that is "quality time" similar to my love language (at the time, I just didn't have a term for the way in which I communicated with the individuals in Haiti), however because I was open-minded, I was able to communicate with those individuals, in a similar way, but since others have a love language that is not similar to mine, I had to be understanding and have a heart of compassion for the other individuals with love languages that are not similar to mine, which I apply in my life every day and during the engagements/communications, that I have with others, because I care about "you".

I also learned many of the individuals, in Haiti did not have money and if an individual did have money, in the terms of an individual I spoke with, "money runs out", I took mental notes and continued to be respectful, open-minded and understanding, in hopes to find a solution one day, because similar to the old saying while sitting in a classroom, no question is considered a stupid question, well this individuals opinion and belief, on how he viewed money was real, and he truly wanted an answer, therefore, I had to know why so I could help him, and I did. I have determined that the solution to "money running out", is to maintain financial security, to then obtain and maintain financial freedom.

My experience in Haiti made me value and appreciate everything and everyone in life. I never viewed materialistic things nor wanted them. I want to find solutions to our major issues our country faces, and create positive innovation within our communities, with "you".

Everyone deserves to be financially free, but in order to do so, you must first be open-minded and understanding of the process to obtain financial freedom, which first requires obtaining financial security.

> *"In order to obtain financial freedom, you must*
> *first obtain financial security"*
> **-Regeline Eden Sabbat**

> *"Prosper in economic times, my fellow warrior"*
> **-Regeline Eden Sabbat**

CHAPTER 7

"Politics"

I truly love politics. Politics is what surrounds our world and holds us together. We are truly the people of the United States.

My experience as an intern for the United States Senate office was life changing. The United States Senate office works hard to make certain every citizen has equal rights. Per the Privacy Act of 1974, my internship communications will remain private, and I will continue to obey the law.

If you ever come across an individual who works in the Senate Office or any government office, please thank them. Respect others the same way you want to be respected. Recall this is the stay focused movement.

Therefore, regarding political views, always remember everyone is obligated to their own opinions.

Make certain to value opinions that are not based on preconceived notions.

As an active member and volunteer in my community, I am filled with so much joy, because when I see the smiles on the faces of the individuals I assist, their smiles are truly remarkable.

I have worked on and volunteered for several campaigns in my community, and I love it.

I always look forward to every election and remaining active in my community. I have volunteered for various campaigns, such as the Marco Rubio campaign, the Carlos Lopez-Cantera campaign (CLS), the Rick Scott campaign, the Ron Desantis and Jeanette Nunez campaign, the Trump campaign, and the RPOF campaigns.

Moreover, I am a James Madison Institute Leaders Fellow Class IV in the Tampa, Florida region, which is a year long program designed for the purpose of encouraging and promoting the growth, development, knowledge, and networks of under 40-year-old professionals in the State of Florida.

Image of the United States of America

Now walk with me and try to complete the map by filling each state below. How many states can you fill in below, and if you can't fill in any states at all without looking back at the map I've provided above, it is fine.

Remember, life is about growing and taking the necessary steps to do so. Therefore, review each state and where it is located on the map above and, then, complete the map below. You can do it! Work on this portion of the book until you can. The time to take action is now!

Every citizen of the United States of America should know where all 50 states are located. Knowing each state's capital is a plus. As citizens of the United States of America, this is our land.

> *"It is significant to know the location of the state you live in, and the locations of each state that surround it. "*
> **-Regeline Eden Sabbat**

What is politics to you?

_____

Where do you obtain your political information from?

_____

Does the source you obtain your political information from lack credibility?

Politics is the activities correlated with the governance of an area or a country. The decisions made in politics apply to members of a group.

The government is the formal institutions and procedures, in which a land and its people (citizens) are ruled.

With the diversity in our country today, regarding the different cultures, our country's politics and its economy has transitioned, and it is now time for all of us to come together and realize this fact, and move forward together.

History matters. However, we don't want to repeat history, therefore, we must not remain focused on the past, or continue discussing matters without the end result being a solution.

Instead, we shall find solutions through the knowledge we have obtained from those past events, and then provide suggestions. Then, change will be implemented. After a suggested solution is reviewed following the proper political procedures (for example, the legislative process-forming an idea into law), then it may be implemented.

We have truly come a long way as a nation. I am proud of the progress I have noticed in our country thus far. Not the progress shown from sources lacking credibility, but the progress I have seen with my own sight, regarding how far we have come as a country by being an active member, volunteering in my community, and following politics closely.

We still have some areas in our country that we have not been able to close the gaps on, because of the emotion's individuals tend to allow to guide their thoughts and actions.

Therefore, it is significant to have a shift in your mindset from a negative mindset of all the negative thoughts that come to mind or that you have seen on television, social media, etc., and maintain a positive mindset to stay focused on the issues at hand. I strongly recommend each citizen do their own research, regarding politics, or a political issue that comes to mind, instead of listening to hearsay. Simply listening to hearsay, is not going to continue the progress our country has worked so hard for. I recommend following politics closely.

Unfortunately, many individuals in our country tend to focus on race when it comes to politics. As a result, the main topics that arise for discussion tend to become diminished, and for those reasons, sadly, right in front of our eyes, our country is slowly remaining as a divided country.

Many individuals want justice and equality regarding politics and the government, but if an individual express themselves through aggression or violence, it is not the answer. Expression through love is the answer, not hate. No one can be heard through hate and anger.

Therefore, if a topic is being discussed, such as race, and the sought outcome is change to avoid feeling excluded, then there should not be an attack on the opposite race when discussed— that is a contradiction and, sadly, the main reason a solution to the racial topics that arise never get solved.

No more blaming others or focusing on how things didn't happen; it's time now to focus on the relevant issues in our country that we can work on together to become a better nation as a whole.

Many individuals believe others should already know what the solution to an issue is, but that is not always the case, so yes sometimes explaining ourselves in depth regarding the issues we are concerned about and the solutions we would like implemented, need to be broken down thoroughly, to make certain the individual or individuals we are speaking to can understand us and our concerns. If it takes time, that's fine, that is a step forward. Being misunderstood by one person does not mean that you will be misunderstood by everyone.

Therefore, always seek to share your thoughts, insights, and solutions to any issues you are concerned about, and do so in the way in which you want to be treated with love.

Public opinions are the attitudes of citizens, regarding political issues, leaders, institutions, and events.

Values/beliefs are the basic principles that shape an individual's opinions about political issues and events.

Political ideology is a set of beliefs that form the general philosophy regarding the role of government.

An opinion is a specific preference on a particular issue. (Everyone is obligated to their own opinion).

Poem *entitled:*

" *Politics*"

*We shall not run from the topic of politics anymore; it is
what brings every citizen in our country together*

We shall not act as though politics does not exist

We shall not listen to hearsay

*We shall express our first amendment rights in a
reasonable and respectful manner*

*We shall have peaceful protest and social
movements, then we will be heard*

We shall love, instead of hate

We shall remain positive, not negative

*We shall focus on moving forward and not
focus on the past*

*Together, we shall find solutions
to the issues in our country*

This land is truly our land

Together, we will walk on our land

No longer will we be divided on domestic issues

*We shall stand together be open-minded and
understanding to each other's opinions
about race, religion, gender, sexuality,
age or other social characteristics*

*We shall understand political efficacy and remain
faithful by understanding each vote matters*

*Together, we will create a better tomorrow for
the next generation and future generations*

Change in our country begins now

-Regeline Eden Sabbat

The three branches of government at a glance:
  Legislative branch
  Executive branch
  Judicial branch

The Legislative branch makes laws.

The Executive branch carries out laws.

The Judicial branch evaluates laws.

Do you know who your elected state and local representatives are?

_____

_____

_____

_____

_____

_____

What are your state's economic regions?

_____

_____

_____

_____

_____

_____

_____

_____

A bill is proposed to legislation and is considered by a legislature each session. A bill becomes law once it is passed through the legislature, and in most cases, approved by the executive.

Campaigns are efforts made by political candidates and their supporters in their pursuit for political office.

Voting is a formal expression of an individual's choice in an activity that involves making a decision on someone or something.

Are you registered to vote?

_____

Voting registration is available at the Supervisor of Elections offices in each county, registration drives, driver's license offices, public assistance offices, veterans' offices, libraries, and by mail. If you are not registered to vote, please remember you matter and your vote matters. Your vote is truly your voice.

North Dakota is the only state that does not require voter registration.

Primary elections are held to vote for each party's candidates for the general election.

General elections are elections in which candidates are voted into offices.

Presidential elections follow a different nominating process. Such as formation of an exploratory committee, fund-raising, campaigning, the party debates, the primaries and caucuses, the convention, the general election campaign, the debates, the November election, the electoral college, and the inauguration.

Everyone's vote in the community matters. Your voice matters.

Do you know the preamble to the United States Constitution?

_____
_____
_____
_____
_____
_____

The Preamble to the United States Constitution:

We the People of the United States, in Order to form a more perfect Union, establish Justice, insure domestic Tranquility, provide for the common defense, promote the general Welfare, and secure the Blessings of Liberty to ourselves and our Posterity, do ordain and establish this Constitution for the United States of America.

At a Glance:
The Preamble to the United States Constitution:

We, the People of the United States, in order to form a more perfect union, must start with fairness, protect the peace in our home/our land, provide for the protection of our country as a whole against foreign attack, promote the concern of the government in regards to health, peace, mortality, and safety of its citizens/individuals, and secure the blessings of liberty to ourselves and future generations. Liberty being our country allowing every individual to be free within society/our land, and protected from oppressive/harsh restrictions imposed by authority on ourselves, such as society's standards on what our behavior or political views, etc. should be, and our future generations, we appoint and start this Constitution for the United States of America.

Stay Focused: Many times, the term " posterity", which means future generations, in the Preamble to the United States Constitution tends to get misconstrued with "prosperity", which means the state of being wealthy/rich. For these reasons, we must secure the blessings of liberty to ourselves and future generations, by staying focused and taking action together by sharing positive ideas to form positive innovation in our country.

What is the United States Bill of Rights? _____

_____

_____

_____

What is an Amendment?

Amendments: _____

_____

_____

_____

Amendments are an insertion or a change to a statute, constitution, or legislative resolution or bill.

Recall, we are on the stay focused movement. Therefore, we must walk together to make certain the reform our country implements is based on the changes we vote on as nation.

Take action, and understand the differences between the two major political parties: the Republican Party and the Democratic Party. Great job! Let's see the knowledge you have obtained from taking action and being active in your community!

_____

_____

_____

_____

_____

_____

_____

_____

_____

_____

_____

_____

_____

_____

_____

_____

_____

_____

_____

_____

_____

_____

_____

_____

_____

Furthermore, we must begin to have discussions on our social media platforms that do not cause hate and that do not lead to hate. For example, if an individual misinterprets a comment when an individual reads a comment and then, that individual believes they have no choice, so they resort to hate as well. No, there is a choice that is positivity and love, not hate. Imagine how many solutions we can find for many issues our country faces today. Imagine if we were to have discussions without one party attacking the other party.

The answer is with positivity. Now, with positive discussions, we will be able to find solutions, by walking together on our social media platforms and walking together in our community. This land is our land, and we must protect it as we walk together. And by respecting each other. How many individuals can say they have a friend who is a "conservative" or a friend who is a "liberal", and the love you and your friend have for each other has remained the same? Why? It is because love always has, and love will forever defeat hate. We must not judge individuals based on their political views.

I am a proud Republican and I have friends who are Democrats with opposite political views and we still love each other the same.

I truly believe bipartisanship matters.

Bipartisanship is when two political parties cooperate, that usually oppose each other's views.

For example, Criminal Justice reform will happen, once Bipartisanship is understood clearly and action is taken in our country and our community to raise awareness on this issue and other issues as well.

It's time to bring our deeply divided country back together. Bipartisanship matters.

Throughout my entire life I have been judged by others in my community for my political views of being a Republican. However, I have not allowed the negative remarks of others to consume my mind with negative remarks. Positivity and facts truly matter. Therefore, I am here to tell you to never allow anyone to alter your decisions based on your political views. However, make certain your political views/votes are based on your own research, that are based on facts, and not misleading information you view in the media. Therefore, when you vote in future elections, make certain you do your own research, and that any information you obtain are based on facts.

Moving forward...

Let's continue to walk together!

We can do it, we must do it, and we will do it!

Republican Party (Allows you to vote in the primary elections):
Hint*Conservative
Right Wing
Red

_____

_____

_____

Democratic Party (Allows you to vote in the primary elections):
Hint*Liberal
Left Wing
Blue

_____

_____

_____

There is a difference between the term "democracy" and the term "democrat".

We shall understand that American democracy is the government of the people. Basically, democracy is a system of government in which the citizens exercise power by voting.

Therefore, each citizen must take action and utilize their right to vote during each election.

The United States has two major political parties: the Republican Party and the Democratic Party.

The United States also has the political parties such as Independent, no party affiliation, etc.

During each election, know all the candidates and their reform policies before voting.

Watch all the debates during the election. Understand each candidate's stance on each political issue.

Take action and vote— your vote matters! You matter! Our country matters! Let's make our better tomorrow happen during each election! Maintain a warrior's mindset. This is truly the stay focused movement.

"For change in our community to be possible, we must take action to understand our voting rights."

Regeline Eden Sabbat

CHAPTER 8

"Sociology"

Sociology is a social science that studies the science of society, patterns of social interaction, social relationships, and the culture in our daily lives. The methods used are critical analysis and factual investigation.

The topics I discuss in this series are education, substance abuse and mental health, and suicide, etc. As we continue to walk together, I want to hear your thoughts and ideas on other aspects/topics of sociology.

Education is significant in our community, because it is the system in which individuals learn and obtain knowledge. The more technology advances in this era, there will be different methods by which individuals learn.

Therefore, it is important for everyone in society to be cautious of how he/she obtains information. Make certain you obtain information from credible sources.

Every individual has the ability to become a leader in our community, and with the knowledge you have, in your area of expertise, being active in your community makes a huge difference. This is truly the stay focused movement. Take action now and be resourceful!

We must raise awareness regarding protecting our environment/ land we live in.

I learned how important our environment was during my environmental law class in UCF, from my amazing Professor Marien. and my amazing friend, Amy Ford. There is more to our environment being the surrounding/conditions in which an individual, animal, or plant lives and operates. I learned sustainability matters. Amy's ideas and thoughts for innovation regarding sustainability are truly remarkable. I am so excited to have her join us on our walk, because together, we will learn about how to sustain our environment from Amy. I am so excited. Until then, please make certain to recycle. We must protect and maintain our environment in a positive and healthy manner.

My Best friend Amy and I

It is truly amazing how we will raise awareness regarding major issues in our community through education.

Mental health is our cognitive, emotional, psychological, behavioral, and social well-being. According to the National Institute of Mental Health, research has shown that mental illnesses are common in the United States, and it affects tens of millions of people each year.

Sadly, many individuals with a mental illness do not receive treatment. To obtain more information regarding the different types of mental illnesses, please visit the website https://www.nimh.nih.gov/health/statistics/mental-illness.shtml

We must raise awareness regarding mental health.

We must raise awareness on the Second Amendment, which is the right of the people to keep and bear arms, and per our constitution, that right shall not be infringed. However, we must find a solution to reduce gun violence, not remove an individual's rights to bear arms. Based on the precedent incidents that have taken place, they have been due to the mental health of an individual or a lack of a thorough background check when the individual purchased the gun.

We must raise awareness regarding bullying and find solutions to take positive action that will lead to effective results, and positive change in the deviant behavior of an individual who bullies another individual. We must protect every individual in our country.

We must raise awareness on epilepsy (purple heart).

We must raise awareness of abuse in nursing homes and skilled nursing home facilities.

We must raise awareness of all abuse.

We must raise awareness on Sexual Assault.

We must raise awareness on Domestic Violence.

We must raise awareness on Human Trafficking.

We must raise awareness on financial literacy, and have it taught in our education systems.

We must raise awareness on the subjects/courses taught in our educational systems/ private schools (education reform).

We must raise awareness on the opioid crisis.

We must raise awareness on teaching the difference between pro-life and pro-choice.

We must raise awareness on entrepreneurship and what it means. Entrepreneurship is the process of designing, launching, and operating a new business, which is often initially a small business. Moreover, individuals who create those businesses are called entrepreneurs.

We must raise awareness on criminal justice reform. And, we must reduce the recidivism rate.

We must raise awareness on all types of cancer, including breast cancer.

We must raise awareness on International Relations.

We must raise awareness on Veterans Affairs.

We must raise awareness of individuals with intellectual and developmental disabilities.

We must raise awareness on LGBT + Rights.

We must raise awareness on Kidney Disease Research.

We must raise awareness on Cerebral Palsy.

We must raise awareness on Spina Bifida.

We must raise awareness on the missing child alerts in our community and remaining vigilant in our community.

We must raise awareness on Vaping Dangers & Public Health.

We must raise awareness on Infrastructure Reform.

We must raise awareness on taxes.

We must raise awareness on employment reform.

We must raise awareness on housing affordability for every individual (For students and graduates as well).

We must raise awareness on Health & Nutrition.

We must raise awareness of animal cruelty.

We must raise awareness on Natural Disaster Evacuation Safety Preparation Requirements.

We must raise awareness on assisting with recovery efforts in our community, after natural disasters occur in our community.

I understand individuals will take action and ask for help, if they know there is someone who cares, that they can speak with. Therefore, I have provided the contact information for the major issues in our community today. If you or an individual needs assistance regarding any of the matters I have listed below, please contact the number provided below to receive assistance:

National Suicide Prevention Lifeline
Call 1-800-273-TALK (8255); En Español 1-888-628-9454

Crisis Text Line
Text "HELLO" to 741741

Veterans Crisis Line
Call 1-800-273-TALK (8255) and press 1 or text to 838255

Disaster Distress Helpline
Call 1-800-985-5990 or text "TalkWithUs" to 66746

Please contact 911 immediately in an emergency.

Suicide is self-inflicted death. An individual can obtain confidential help by contacting the National Suicide Prevention line:1-800-273-8255

National Suicide Prevention Lifeline
Call 1-800-273-TALK (8255); En Español 1-888-628-9454

According to the National Institute on Drug Abuse (Advancing Addiction Science), more than 130 people in the United States die after overdosing on opioids. This is a serious national crisis. Please visit the following website for more information: https://www.drugabuse.gov/drugs-abuse/opioids/opioid-overdose-crisis

The Substance Abuse And Mental Health Services Aministration/ SAMHSA National Helpline (also known as the treatment Referral Routing Service). SAMHSA is available everyday at any time:1(800)-662-4357. Individuals will receive assistance in regards to mental and/or substance use disorders. SAMHSA also provides referrals to local support groups, treatment facilities, and community-based organizations.

The Power and control wheel provided by the domestic abuse intervention project National Domestic Violence Hotline at 1–800–799–7233 or TTY 1–800–787–3224

For those of you who have been through domestic violence or another hardship, with the knowledge or insight you gain from my book please realize that you are not what happened to you in any situation, but you too have dreams and goals that are still obtainable, no matter what traumatic event/serious hardship you are faced with in your life. Always remember your experiences, circumstances, or challenges don't define you. You matter and your life matters. Remember, a positive mindset/a warrior's mindset equals results. You are a warrior. However, always remember forgiveness matters.

The lesson here, is to always proceed in your life with a positive mindset of never giving up, no matter what.

A women/individual had been through a traumatic event/ serious hardship, while enrolled in law school, which prohibited her from performing at her normal level, and despite everything she had been through, she overcame this major challenge in her life, and now she is attending a different law school, not because of a lack of capacity for the study of law, but because of a traumatic event/serious hardship, that prohibited her from performing at her normal level. I share this information with you because, that women is me. Always remember, true warriors never give up. Keep going! And, keep in mind forgiveness matters.

> *"Once you take the first step towards a healthier life, you won't ever want to go back, only forward."*
> **- Regeline Eden Sabbat**

Only Forward

CHAPTER 9

"Networking"

Networking is amazing and significant to do in your community, because you are able to connect with other individuals.

Whether an individual is like-minded or not you are able to exchange information, regarding what you do, and it is an opportunity for both of you to learn about each other.

Many of my great friends have come from networking events. My business network has expanded, because of the business connections I have made, and the services I have provided in the various fields I have skills and experience for, and I love it. My passion is truly helping others any way that I can.

In this era that we live in today, it is amazing at how many different ways we can network, we do not just have social media platforms that are available in the areas we live in, where we physically have to attend. Now, we have networking apps, such as Shapr, Bumble Bizz, etc.

It is truly amazing. I definitely recommend networking in your community. Take action today.

The longer you wait, that is one less connection that you could have just made.

Once you are at a networking event or you are socializing with someone, make certain when you arrive at the networking event you are not just handing out business cards, but you are engaging with individuals and communicating with individuals when they come up to you, or when you both have the opportunity to meet.

Exchanging business cards during a conversation while networking is great, but while you do so do not forget the most beautiful aspect of networking, which is to build relationships.

If you are networking and engaging with someone on a social media platform or on an app such as Shapr, Bumble Bizz, etc make certain that you approach the conversation in a respectful manner and not start a conversation off with a sales pitch or a script.

Instead approach the conversation with a greeting and actually be engaged in the conversation, not just responding to get to a point in your favor. It is amazing once we get to know others for whom they truly are aside from their job title, how we can build a business relationship, that may lead to a business collaboration, friendship, or you may assist each other with the services you each provide. Another amazing outcome of networking is the ideas you exchange with others and how those ideas may help others, if those ideas were put into action. Overall, treat others with respect. You can do it.

Take action today. Look at some of the networking events in your area and plan to go. Either this week or weekend and plan to go.

I am sure you are wondering where to start networking.

For starters, you now know of two networking apps. On social media platforms such as Facebook it provides users with a list of networking events in their area.

Let's Review:

What is networking?

_____

_____

_____

What are some of the various ways you can network?

_____

_____

_____

What networking apps are currently available?

_____

_____

How many networking events have you been to in your community?

_____

If you have attended a networking event in your community, how many new relationships did you make, that you will build on?

_____

_____

How do you plan to stay in touch with an individual you meet while networking?

_____

_____

Do you recall the name of the individuals you spoke with at the last networking event you attended? If not, what are some ways you can improve your communication and active listing skills?

_____

_____

_____

What type of networking events are you interested in attending this year?

_____

_____

_____

What is the next networking event you will attend?

_____

Absolutely Amazing! I am so proud of you!

Take action today! Enjoy networking in your community!

CHAPTER 10

"Obtain a Mentor"

Obtaining a mentor is truly significant, because essentially what you are doing is you are saying, Hey! I am in a position right now where I need assistance in a particular area in my life.

Similar to the way an individual looking to become physically fit, who feels as though they are not physically fit, will obtain a personal fitness trainer. Then, the outcome is the individual receives fitness assistance and obtains more knowledge regarding their own health and nutrition, to become physically fit.

Another example let's say an individual feels as though they are not financially fit, then that individual will obtain a financial representative to become financially fit. Then, the outcome is the individual receives financial assistance and obtains more knowledge regarding financial literacy.

For these reasons, I highly recommend obtaining a mentor who can assist you and provide you with the knowledge you will utilize, to go to the next level. The worst thing you can do, is obtain a mentor who will have you in the same position you were in when you started. For example, if you begin receiving assistance to obtain financial freedom, but you are still financially in debt and do not have financial security, then this is an example of the type of mentorship you should not keep.

Make certain, when you receive mentorship advice that you see progress in your life. However, it is also significant to understand, every mentor seeks to help their mentee as much as they can. Therefore, sometimes we have to look in the mirror, and determine where we may need to reevaluate a few things ourselves, because sometimes we need to change a few things and make readjustments in our own lives, and not blame our mentor, because that is an excuse. Change is always possible, but we must first allow ourselves to accept change into our lives, because with change, we will see results. Therefore, change begins with "you". Prior to obtaining a mentor ask yourself, are you willing to be open minded and are you committed to reaching your goals, because if you are, in order to obtain results, you must first accept the process of change.

For example, I love my mentorship I received from my mentor Andy Audate, because my journey with his mentorship began when I was an attendee at his Progression Conference on April 27th, 2019 and the next thing I know, I am on tour with him. I went on tour with Andy to Houston,Texas and Dallas, Texas. Both Progression Conferences were back to back. I definitely saw progress because I went from being an attendee at his Progression Conference in Los Angeles, California on April 27th, 2019 to becoming a speaker at his Progression Conference on August 23rd, 2019 (Dallas, Texas) and August 24th, 2019 (Houston,Texas).

I spoke at his Progression Conference in Dallas, Texas and Houston, Texas after I completed his Elite Presenters Academy. I'll always remember and cherish the moment, my mentor Andy told me " I believe in you, Regeline".

Progression Conference Attendee- April 27th, 2019

Progression Conference Tour- (Dallas and Houston, Texas 2019).

My mentor Andy is truly amazing because he helped me every step of the way and when I had questions, he was there to help me. I told Andy, " I do not ask for assistance or ask questions often, but when I do, it is because I have tried every way possible to figure it out myself, and then when I cannot that is when I reach out for assistance, because I take into consideration that you are a hardworking and busy individual. I'll never forget when he told me, "I understand you Regeline, and that it is fine, contact me anytime you need assistance, because I am here to help you." I am truly grateful for my mentorship. This is an example; of the type of mentorship you should obtain and keep.

Today, I can definitely say "I see the progression in my life." Even though it was accelerated progression, Andy's mentorship exceeded my expectations.

Andy's mentorship through his Elite Presenters Academy, got me out of my comfort zone, regarding the speaking skills I already had, because now my network has expanded enormously.

Since my accelerated transition through the mentorship I obtained, I am able to live my dreams and help others by sharing the knowledge I have obtained throughout the years with my Bachelor of Arts degree in Political Science-Pre law and Sociology, and the experience, skills, and knowledge I obtained in various fields such as social work, politics, law and government, interpreting (Haitian Creole and French), customer service/hospitality, the financial industry, and entrepreneurship. Teaching with a heart of compassion, utilizing effective listening and communication skills matters.

Multi-skilled individuals do exist, and with strong leaders such as "you", yes "you", we will create positive innovation our world needs, by continuing to walk together. Helping each other by using our effective listening skills and communication skills to collaborate our ideas, to then implement positive change in our community.

This effective approach when collaborating with others, will help others become amazing leaders, and then those amazing leaders can help others become amazing leaders, who will focus on the solutions for the major issues in our country and community, that benefit our community and country for the better as the "United Nation", we will become. A united nation our founding fathers would be so proud of. The first step is to truly believe, and once you believe it will happen, it will. Let's continue to walk together in our country and community.

Do you have a mentor?

_____

If, not take action now and obtain one! You can do it!

What is the name of the mentor you obtained?

_____

This is truly, exciting news. I am so happy for you. Great job on taking action to obtain a mentor, I knew you could do it!

As the amazing quote by Bob Proctor states

"A mentor is someone who sees more talent and ability within you, then you see in yourself, and helps bring it out of you. "

Faith can move mountains - Matthew 17:20

CHAPTER 11

"Infinite Mountains"

When faced with a new challenge/mountain to climb, always remember no matter how high or how far the end may seem, it's not over yet it's just the beginning, because the reality is once you reach the top of one mountain, a task that once seemed as the main accomplishment or goal will accumulate to another mountain, and then another mountain, because we are designed to strive for more in our lifetimes. Therefore, we will be faced with infinite mountains in our lives.

For example, think of when you were young you wanted to be an adult, then when you became an adult you wished you never said you wanted to be an adult, when you were 15 you wished you could be 16 already, and you may have even counted the days down, but the truth of the matter is when you finally passed your exam to obtain your driver's license, and you drove very often, after a while you most likely wondered why you ever thought it would be fun, and when you graduated high school you were very excited to attend college, only to determine, once you got to college you didn't expect for it to be as difficult as it was, and when you graduated college, you thought amazing things were going to happen instantly, and that you were going to have the job of your dreams, only to realize nothing in this lifetime is handed to you, you have to go and get it, everything you want and desire you have to go after as if there was no tomorrow, and work hard.

The list of mountains I have mentioned above could go on, and the truth of the matter is that the mountains will always be there, you just have to realize that they are there, but the question is how bad do you want to reach your dreams?

No one is going to climb the mountain for you, and no there are not any elevators to get to the top of this mountain you are attempting to climb at the moment, but remember you have climbed mountains before, therefore what is stopping you from climbing a mountain you are faced with in any area of your life at this moment?

Now that you can look at the mountains as being infinite instead of one after the other, then I have faith and I believe you will climb this mountain and you will reach the top, but this time when you get to the top of this mountain you won't stop for a few days, or a few months, or years even, because now you know what to expect. Therefore, go after your dreams and don't just chase them, reach each and every one of your dreams, because you can, and you will.

The plans God has destined for you no one can take from you. Remember that.

For I know the plans I have for you, declares the Lord, plans to
prosper you and not to harm you, plans to give you hope
and a future

Jeremiah 29:11

CHAPTER 12

"Let's Continue to Walk Together"

The time has come now, where you have completed the first steps of the blueprint for the warrior's mindset and our stay focused movement, we have embarked on. Absolutely amazing! I am so proud of you! I am truly excited to continue to walk with everyone on our journey, in our country, it's "because of you" that the stay focused movement is even possible.

Together, we will make positive and effective innovations in our community.

Together we will now be active listeners and observers, in our community and help each other along the way, to not only reach our goals, but to help others in our community/country reach their goals, and to set the precedent for the future-generation. This is truly exciting, and it all starts with us "walking together".

America is truly our country! I am so excited, because there are so many ways we can conquer/innovate negative aspects in our community, and convert those negative aspects into positive aspects, as we continue walking together and give back to our community. Walking together is beautiful!

Walking together is truly possible, because everyone is unique and everyone brings a unique characteristic to the table or on our path, everyone is a unique warrior. Being "You" is truly beautiful, because being "You", truly makes "You" unique and wonderful. You have the knowledge and creativity to implement your ideas. Your ideas matter. You matter.

Therefore, let's continue to walk together and remain open-minded to our ideas, valuing and appreciating the diversity in our country. Let's be active leaders in our community, because together anything is possible. We can, we will, and we must, because there is an individual out there who is waiting for "us", where they are now currently in their lives, so they too can continue to walk with us, someone out there is waiting, imagine that.

Imagine you waiting! What may have happened, if I did not come out and walk with you? There is an individual in our country with ideas just like you and is ready to take action but does not know where to start. Once we walk together, that individual will join us, because the individual will realize they matter too. Everyone matters!

Let's continue walking together and moving forward in our country. No more looking in the rearview mirror, only forward.

Our purpose on our walk is to raise awareness. Awareness+Intervention/ Positive Action=Prevention/Solutions.

Together, we will make positive and effective innovations in our country and community.

Together we will now be active listeners and observers, in our country and community, and help each other along the way, to not only reach our goals, but to help others in our country and community to reach their goals too, and to set the precedent for the future-generation. This is truly exciting, and it all starts with us "walking together".

America is truly our Nation! I am so excited, because there are so many ways, we can conquer negative aspects in our country and community, and convert those negative aspects into positive aspects, as we continue walking together and give back to our community. Walking together is beautiful!

Walking together is truly possible, because everyone is unique and everyone brings a unique characteristic to the table or on our path, everyone is a unique warrior. Being "You" is truly beautiful, because being "You", truly makes "You" unique and wonderful. You have the knowledge and creativity to implement your ideas. Your ideas matter. You matter. Therefore, be free and be you.

Therefore, let's continue to walk together and remain open-minded to our ideas, valuing and appreciating the diversity in our country and community. Let's be active leaders in our community, because together anything is possible. We can, we will, and we must, because there is an individual out there who is waiting for "us", where they are now currently in their lives, so they too can continue to walk with us, someone out there is waiting, imagine that.

Imagine you waiting! What may have happened, if I did not come out and walk with you? There is an individual in our country with ideas just like you and is ready to take action but does not know where to start. Once we walk together, that individual will join us, because the individual will realize they matter too. Everyone matters!

Now, let's continue walking together and move forward in our country and community. No more looking in the rearview mirror, only forward my fellow warrior.

Our purpose on our walk is to raise awareness.
Awareness+Intervention/Positive Action=Prevention/Solutions.

"Together Innovation is truly possible."

- Regeline Eden Sabbat

I am truly a woman of God, an individual of faith, a warrior of christ, I am staying focused and I will continue walking with other individuals. Together, we will Innovate our world and it will reflect the beautiful world God (or the person or thing) you believe in created for everyone.

Let's continue walking together and move forward in our country and community. No more looking in the rearview mirror, only forward.

Our purpose on our walk is to raise awareness.
Awareness+Intervention/Positive Action=Prevention/Solutions.

Growing is truly the beauty of life. No matter what challenges may come on your path during this lifetime, always remember God (or the person or thing) you believe in, is truly with you every step of the way. Therefore, continue to move forward and focus on your priorities and the things that mean the world to "you" during this "one lifetime." **Regeline Eden Sabbat**

"Believe in yourself and never give up on yourself."
-Regeline Eden Sabbat

**The Stay Focused Movement
Only Forward**

CPSIA information can be obtained
at www.ICGtesting.com
Printed in the USA
LVHW080011260620
658989LV00029B/1183